# Notebook 19

# Notebook 19

Poems by

Dennis J. Bernstein

© 2023 Dennis J. Bernstein. All rights reserved.
This material may not be reproduced in any form, published,
reprinted, recorded, performed, broadcast,
rewritten or redistributed without
the explicit permission of Dennis J. Bernstein.
All such actions are strictly prohibited by law.

Cover design by Shay Culligan
Author photo by Jennifer Hasegawa

ISBN: 978-1-63980-298-2
Library of Congress Control Number: 2023934687

Kelsay Books
502 South 1040 East, A-119
American Fork, Utah 84003
Kelsaybooks.com

For Jennifer Hasegawa / through all of it together.

# THE FIRST NIGHT
## *NOTEBOOK 19:*

*Foreword by Jack Foley, award-winning poet and critic*

There is a spectre haunting these poems but it is not the spectre Marx and Engels saw haunting Europe in the famous first sentence of The Manifesto of the Communist Party. That document goes on, "All the powers of old Europe have entered into a holy alliance to exorcise this spectre . . ."

The spectre of this book is Covid-19 and it is not the powers of old Europe that are seeking to exorcise it, but the powers of the whole world.

Because of Dennis Bernstein's brilliant investigative journalism on Berkeley radio station KPFA, people tend to think of him as deeply involved in the world of politics, but it is equally true that he is deeply involved in the world beyond politics as well. In this book, it is the world as such that is in question. "The phone keeps ringing," he writes,

even after I answer it,
even after I pull it out of the wall
and throw it out the window.

These poems, these cris de coeur, are a mixture of anguish and despair and perhaps, in a complex way—if only because they are poems—of hope. They move us in different, always problematical, directions, sometimes autobiographical, sometimes surreal, sometimes passionately direct: "Over 70 and compromised."

What can we do when "the enemy" is not Old Man Capitalism—which is a real enough enemy—but something simultaneously ubiquitous, invisible, and deadly?

This book is the powerful account of the consciousness we have entered as we enter the 21st century. It does not show us how to defeat the enemy. It is only a powerful mirror of how we must live with and within it, of the suffering it brings. It is not a mode of criticism but a mode of remembering. It is the tremendous and deeply affecting cry of a historical moment:

Death from a distance. Our smallest moves must
make all the difference: I am forbidden from touching
your face but I can still peer into your fierce blue eyes.

# Contents

I.

| | |
|---|---|
| Dark Awakenings | 15 |
| Pertinent Fact (19) in 2019 | 16 |
| The New Bomb Shelter Is a Vaccine | 17 |
| COVID WHISPERS | 18 |
| Viral Novel | 19 |
| The Terror of Early Morning Dailyness | 20 |
| Love and Death in the Age of 19 | 21 |
| Safe Travel | 22 |
| Novel Honors | 23 |
| Radio Robert Goes Silent | 24 |
| The Covid Coroner | 25 |
| Bells for the Pandemic | 26 |
| Touch | 27 |
| Shortfall | 28 |
| Dark Hints | 29 |
| Kids in the Borderlands | 30 |
| Out of My Pen Point | 31 |
| Versed Aid | 32 |
| Escape Route | 33 |
| Fractured Dreams | 34 |
| Covid Blockage | 35 |
| The New Porno— | 36 |
| Pandemic Pastime | 37 |
| Last Looks | 38 |
| Ten Lashes | 39 |
| Valentine's Day Massacre | 40 |
| The Novel Spread | 41 |
| Final Pointers | 42 |
| Old Habits Immune to the Virus | 43 |

II.

| | |
|---|---|
| Timeshares | 47 |
| Pre-Occupation | 48 |
| (Dis)Connections | 49 |
| Time Frames | 50 |
| Chest Pains | 51 |
| Hospice Notes: | 52 |
| Homeschooling in the Age of 19 | 53 |
| Secret Ammunition | 54 |
| Flight 19 | 55 |
| My Mother's Will | 56 |
| Rain In Your Honor | 57 |
| On the Brink of Drink | 58 |
| Aging Process | 59 |
| Covid Sleep | 60 |
| Covid Poet | 61 |
| In the Age of 19 | 62 |
| Death Spray | 63 |
| United States of Extinction: In Golden Gate Park | 64 |
| Living in Fear of Covid | 65 |
| Flirting with the Afterlife | 66 |
| Time Re-Zoned | 67 |
| Epilogue: A Pandemic Look Back | 69 |
| The Covid Lunatic | 71 |

I.

# Dark Awakenings

I was too sick to touch the moonlight
                        without putting on gloves.

# Pertinent Fact (19) in 2019

The coronavirus has become a political gun for hire.

A few hundred million people tempt death to make a point.

# The New Bomb Shelter Is a Vaccine

In 1963, two countries faced off, poised to end the world.
I was in the eighth grade. My mom was at work some-
where adding up numbers in long columns. My father
was driving hundreds of miles, going nowhere in particular
in his yellow Checker Cab, which was also a front for a floating
gambling den. Meanwhile, I was crouched down in a hallway,
being shushed by a teacher who was telling me to zip it or
the enemy would hear me and know exactly where to drop
the bombs. Now the bombs are silent and the enemy—invisible.

COVID WHISPERS
COVID WHISPERS
COVID WHISPERS
COVID WHISPERS
COVID WHISPERS
COVID WHISPERS
COVID WHISPERS
COVID WHISPERS
COVID WHISPERS
COVID WHISPERS
COVID WHISPERS
COVID WHISPERS
COVID WHISPERS
COVID WHISPERS
COVID WHISPERS
COVID WHISPERS
COVID WHISPERS
COVID WHISPERS
COVID WHISPERS
COVID WHISPERS
COVID WHISPERS
COVID WHISPERS
COVID WHISPERS
COVID WHISPERS
COVID WHISPERS
COVID WHISPERS
COVID WHISPERS
COVID WHISPERS

# Viral Novel

He watches the sun rise
over the morning news—
top of the fold in flames.

# The Terror of Early Morning Dailyness

Here we go again—
and the town street sweeper
fear stalks me. The mitten-
of the virus,    a key below
threatens to repossess

even before the sun makes dawn,
does the rounds,
knuckled kiss
the C of silence,
my name.

# Love and Death in the Age of 19

Our friend is dying.
It is time for the purest
transmissions of love:
from a distance,
the smallest moves
must
make all the difference.

# Safe Travel

I plug my radio into the falling sky—
a few old transistors transport me
into an alternative reality.

# Novel Honors

On the seventh day
he passes; it begins to pour—
breaking a long dry spell
in his honor.

# Radio Robert Goes Silent

Our last time together, we shared
rice cakes and nut butter—hot sake
sent a warm rush up the spine, and
we bathed in starlight,

where

the Russian River returns the sky's
gifts to the sea. Now what's left of
you, my friend: thirty years of taped
voices? You're perfectly invisible,
as always.

# The Covid Coroner

Sorrow Jones lives
on the edge of an eyelid—
a tear shy of drowning.

# Bells for the Pandemic

If my sadness was a bell,
it would never stop ringing—

# Touch

19 leaves me searching between
the lines for what's missing;
there is a kiss, but no lips.
Touch no longer has a say in this.

# Shortfall

These days, I can fit my entire back pocket
into my wallet without having to move
a single dollar bill out of the way.

# Dark Hints

A persistent cough,
I question death's
indiscretion.

# Kids in the Borderlands

They hobble and      stumble—
mumble     like very old men;

One grieving  teenage     mom,
who has tested     positive for 19,

cries out from her knees—   pleads
with God         for asylum.

# Out of My Pen Point

She has pink eyes,
and purple earrings,
and a note from the muse.

# Versed Aid

She takes out a tweezer
and starts pulling splinters
out of my poems.

# Escape Route

As for a proper path through the pandemic—
memory rattles the old images, my mind rebels,
slips out of town on a daydream of possibilities.

# Fractured Dreams

The moon fell out of my pocket
and rolled across the floor of the
crosstown bus. The glowing circle
cracked into little pieces of indirect light.

# Covid Blockage

This fucking demon is sitting
at the tip of my cheap ballpoint—
ink backed up to last week.

# The New Porno—

a lab full of test tubes
violently trading
bodily fluids.

# Pandemic Pastime

Every morning I hide
on the toilet
to read love poems.

## Last Looks

Death from a distance. Our smallest moves must
make all the difference: I am forbidden from touching
your face, but can still peer into your fierce blue eyes.

# Ten Lashes

got caught
under her eyelid
between blinks—
been stuck here
for two years.

# Valentine's Day Massacre

She put a match to my beard
and started toasting marshmallows—
I opened up a fresh can of worms.

# The Novel Spread

Stuck between 1918 and Novel 19—
we study the present with the full-knowledge

that we don't have the slightest idea
where our future is going.

# Final Pointers

Death-bed / daddy
raffles / off
directions

for the rest / of my life.
He addresses /
me

like I'm / a stranger
on a street /
corner

asking / him
for directions /
to the mall.

# Old Habits Immune to the Virus

He was so used to his daddy's daily beating,
he kept beating himself up for months
after the old man passed on.

II.

# Timeshares

I rented a room
in a tomorrow
that never came.

# Pre-Occupation

Over 70 and compromised—
Death's army gathering
outside my windowsill.

# (Dis)Connections

The phone keeps ringing
even after I answer it,
even after I pull it out of the wall
and throw it out the window.

# Time Frames

I went
to sleep
and
woke
up
a few
months
later
without
missing
a day's
work.

# Chest Pains

Just enough
to give death
a place at the table.

# Hospice Notes:

PARALLEL STRUCTURE
Tonight, my mother's nightmares
are being cared for by the hospice nurse.
I'm listening, out back, to a couple of anxious crows
yapping it up over the corpse of a fallen pigeon.

UNTOUCHABLE
My mother is dying.
I am given gloves to wear
each time before we hug.
Every time I put them on,
she dies a little more.

WHOEVER IS NEXT
Please say goodbye before—
it may be some time before we have
a chance to sit and chat again.

# Homeschooling in the Age of 19

Take our ten-day online Crash Course, HOME VISITS. Learn how to perform ten of the most common surgeries on your own dining room table. Learn how to fill your own cavities, catheterize your hubby's ticker and replace a hip or two. You can even take out your own tonsils without missing a virtual day at the office.

# Secret Ammunition

Saliva loads the gun
in our mouths—the virus
uses a silencer.

# Flight 19

Mother is leaving us.
She takes off
from a covert airstrip
underneath her ICU bed:
I hear her engines
coughing on the runway.

# My Mother's Will

We made out her will at six feet.
It's going to be simple, Mom assures me,
I'm giving you everything except the virus—
I'm saving that for your father in hell.

# Rain In Your Honor

On the seventh day after your death,

it begins to pour—breaking a long

dry spell in your honor. When the rains pass,

I freshen the flowers around your grave, leave

a tall glass of water on top of your stone

in case you grow thirsty

through the long night.

# On the Brink of Drink

Thinking so hard—
my aunt's Sloe Gin Fizz
explodes in her hands.

# Aging Process

learning
how
to
count
to
ten
on
nine
fingers

# Covid Sleep

Dulled by ALZHEIMER'S and 19—
yet he has twenty-twenty vision
and a perfect memory in every dream.

# Covid Poet

The unconscious
does most of the editing now.
I see it happening
in the center
of my floating brain.
I see the cross-outs
effortlessly

disappearing
and the replacements
fitting perfectly into place—
like a finely tailored
three-piece suit.

# In the Age of 19

You shake hands,
the hand behind your back—
shaking.

# Death Spray

They shouted at each other
over white corn and cantaloupe
in the produce section: No masks!

# United States of Extinction: In Golden Gate Park

Mr. buffalo & I are pondering the pandemic—
standing perfectly still—
trying to remember what

life used to be like before a million
of us (and almost every buffalo
in the Western Hemisphere)

were quietly cut down by a Novel
Corona—backed up by an unlimited
supply of gunpowder.

# Living in Fear of Covid

It took me three years
to open up the front door
and check the mailbox.

# Flirting with the Afterlife

Death made another pass at me
today: much more compelling than his last.

# Time Re-Zoned

Now
is
the
time
you
have
never
known.

What will you do with it?

# Epilogue: A Pandemic Look Back

There we were in 2020, locked down to save our lives, in the middle of a war against an invisible enemy and a looming depression on the horizon—with a maniac at the helm. Historically, an almost picture-perfect return to the conditions of the flu pandemic of 1918.

I have read so much over the years about the 1918 global outbreak and how it terrorized the world, and ravaged entire countries, while claiming more people than WWI. Now, this latest outbreak claims the same fame. I wanted to know everything about the 1918 scourge because my father was never far from the pain of losing his mother to it, a moment after he was born. "Her last breath gave me my first," he said. I felt blessed that I was not subjected to this sort of threat, from an enemy that no army in history, no matter how mighty—could counter: A fighting force of microscopic killers that struck down millions without warning or mercy.

And now, here we are again, locked down (with our 21$^{st}$ century technology), ducking in and out of doorways, doing our shopping on the sly, or online, all of us becoming anti-touch people in a world made for touch. Can you make love from six feet? How about a six-foot hug, or a nice long kiss, two yards away from my hips and lips?

Oh, and of course there's death and life at a distance; does that new mother skip the first bonding and kiss, in an attempt to avoid the kiss of death? And what can one say, how might we endure that six-foot spread, when I'm over here, masked, shielded and gloved, and you are dying by the second, your breaths uneven, fewer and further in-between. The distance and the disease kill us. You die: your distant death stuck in my eyes.

I am grateful that my daddy didn't have to endure this triple-threat war against an enemy that can tiptoe in from any angle and take you down where you stand. I guess it's a selfish thought, but as I look out of my city window—where folks in masks, with kids in masks, some without masks—wait for their turn in line for the cash machine, and I am too sad to cry or rage. But the big silver lining of this deadly cloud is that daddy is not being forced to live underneath it, never knowing when the poison rain might take his son or granddaughter. Last night, I dreamt he had us all locked in a room as he stood outside like a World War II sentry, ready to die for the last thing he believed in.

# The Covid Lunatic

So happy in the graveyard
with mommy and daddy.
I laugh and weep like a lunatic—
share a plate of greens
with an aging hare.

# About the Author

Dennis J. Bernstein is an award-winning poet. His most recent volume, *Five Oceans in a Teaspoon,* won the 2020 IPPY Gold Medal Award for Poetry and the American Bookfest 2020 Best Book Award for Poetry. The book was also a finalist for Poetry International's 2020 Best Book Award. Bernstein's previous collection, *Special Ed: Voices from a Hidden Classroom,* won the 2012 Artists Embassy International Literary Cultural Award. His poetry has appeared in The New York Quarterly, Bat City Review, Texas Observer, ZYZZYVA, and numerous other journals. Bernstein's artist books/plays *French Fries* and *GRRRHHHH: A Study of Social Patterns,* co-authored with Warren Lehrer, are considered seminal works in the genre, and are in the collections of the Museum of Modern Art, the Georges Pompidou Centre, and many other museums around the world. Bernstein is also an award-winning, nationally syndicated host of the news show Flashpoints on Pacifica Radio. His articles and essays have appeared widely in print, including in *The New York Times, Newsday, The Boston Globe,* the *San Francisco Chronicle,* and internationally in *Der Spiegel* and the *Kyoto Journal.*

Made in the USA
Columbia, SC
27 April 2023